TREASURES
FROM THE LOOM

Text and photographs by Katacha Diaz

Daniel and Eleazar Martínez live with their family
in a small town in New Mexico.
They like to ride their horses
and play with their dog, Lobo.
And they like to do something else,
something wonderful.

Daniel and Eleazar are weavers.

The two boys come from a long family line of weavers.

Their great, great, great, great, great-grandfather

was a weaver. He settled in New Mexico

more than 200 years ago.

Many members of his family

still live there.

They farm the land,

tend their sheep, and weave.

The boys' mother taught them how to weave.

Eleazar learned to weave when he was five years old.

Daniel was even younger when he learned.

Both boys have practiced long and hard.

Now their hands fly as they slide the shuttle between the threads.

Their grandfather made the looms they use.

They are like the looms people used hundreds of years ago.

The two brothers weave beautiful designs.

Some designs are old family patterns.

Others are their very own.

Their style of weaving is more than

400 years old.

To color their yarn, the boys make dyes

from old family recipes.

They use plants, rocks, vegetables, and even bugs!

The family gets together to pick

flowers and twigs that grow in the desert.

They will boil these yellow blossoms

to make bright yellow or gold dyes.

The best red dye comes from bugs
that live on one kind of cactus in Mexico.
Daniel and Eleazar buy their bugs at a craft store.
They use a stone to grind the silver-gray bugs
into a fine, red powder.

The boys dye their yarn in big pots
and hang it on a line to dry.
The red-brown dye they are using comes
from a tree root.
When it dries, the yarn
will be ready for weaving.

When school is out, the boys weave.

They make place mats, coasters,

wall hangings, and table runners.

In July, they sell their work

at the big craft market in the city.

It is a time to earn money and have fun.

One year, the governor of New Mexico

and his wife saw the boys' work.

They ordered a set of place mats

to use on their table.

Eleazar and Daniel earn money and prizes
with their weaving.
They have fun, too. Best of all,
they are keeping a family tradition alive
as they weave treasures from the loom.
"Weaving," the brothers say, "is in our blood."